Phonics Focus: vowel +

THE BIRD GIRL

BY CHRISTINA EARLEY

ILLUSTRATED BY
BELLA RECH

A Blue Marlin Book

Introduction:

Phonics is the relationship between letters and sounds. It is the foundation for reading words, or decoding. A phonogram is a letter or group of letters that represents a sound. Students who practice phonics and sight words become fluent word readers. Having word fluency allows students to build their comprehension skills and become skilled and confident readers.

Activities:

BEFORE READING

Use your finger to underline the key phonogram in each word in the *Words to Read* list on page 3. Then, read the word. For longer words, look for ways to break the word into smaller parts (double letters, word I know, ending, etc.).

DURING READING

Use sticky notes to annotate for understanding. Write questions, make connections, summarize each page after it is read, or draw an emoji that describes how you felt about different parts.

AFTER READING

Share and discuss your sticky notes with an adult or peer who also read the story.

Key Word/Phonogram: bird

Words to Read:

fir	birdsong	squirrels
sir	birthday	sunbird
birch	birthstone	tapirs
bird	bluebird	thirsty
chirp	chirping	thirteenth
first	circle	thirty
girl	cowbird	Virden
irg	giraffes	zircon
irks	Irma	admiral
shirt	Irwin	birdwatching
skirt	redbird	Hiroshi
smirk	seabird	hummingbird
squirm	Shirley	Irvington
whirl	skirmish	piranha
birdman	songbird	

Irma is a girl who loves birds. Today is her thirteenth birthday.

She wears her favorite shirt and matching skirt. She puts on her special blue zircon necklace. It has her birthstone.

Irma meets her friend Shirley at Hiroshi Park to go birdwatching. First, they notice a cowbird whirl in the sky.

"I see a hummingbird on a branch," says Shirley.

"I think that's a sunbird," says Irma with a smirk.

"Those squirrels near the birch tree are in a skirmish! That irks me," says Irma.

"I hear something," Shirley says. "What bird makes that chirp?"

"It could be a redbird or a bluebird," says Irma. "Let's go ask the birdman near the fir tree."

"Sir, what bird is chirping?" asks Irma.

"Hello, girls," the birdman says politely. "My name is Admiral Virden. You are hearing the birdsong of a redbird. I know lots about birds. I once saw a seabird circle a piranha."

"Irg! That makes me squirm," says Irma.

"Me, too," says Shirley. "I'm thirsty. Let's go to the Songbird Café."

"Happy Birthday!" shout thirty people.

"Wow! What a surprise," says Irma.

"For my birthday, I want to go to the Irvington Zoo," says Irma's brother Irwin.

"What a great idea!" says Irma. "We could see tapirs and giraffes. And lots of birds, of course!"

Quiz:

1. **True or false?** Irma's birthstone is blue zircon.
2. **True or false?** It is Irma's tenth birthday.
3. **True or false?** The surprise party is for Shirley.
4. What is the genre of the story? What clues tell you?
5. What do you think would be a good job for Irma? Why?

Flip the book around for answers!

Answers:
1. True
2. False
3. False
4. Possible answer: Realistic fiction, because it is a pretend story about events that could happen in real life.
5. Possible answer: She would make a good veterinarian for birds because she loves birds.

Activities:

1. Write a story about Irwin's day at Irvington Zoo.

2. Write a new story using some or all of the "ir" words from this book.

3. Create a vocabulary word map for a word that was new to you. Write the word in the middle of a paper. Surround it with a definition, illustration, sentence, and other words related to the vocabulary word.

4. Make a song to help others learn the sound of "ir."

5. Design a game to practice reading and spelling words with "ir."

Written by: Christina Earley
Illustrated by: Bella Rech
Design by: Rhea Magaro-Wallace
Editor: Kim Thompson
Educational Consultant: Marie Lemke, M.Ed.
Series Development: James Earley

Library of Congress PCN Data
The Bird Girl (ir) / Christina Earley
Blue Marlin Readers
ISBN 979-8-8873-5296-1 (hard cover)
ISBN 979-8-8873-5381-4 (paperback)
ISBN 979-8-8873-5466-8 (EPUB)
ISBN 979-8-8873-5551-1 (eBook)
Library of Congress Control Number: 2022951106

Printed in the United States of America.

Seahorse Publishing Company
seahorsepub.com

Copyright © 2024 **SEAHORSE PUBLISHING COMPANY**

All rights reserved. No part of this publication may be reproduced, stored in a retrieval system or be transmitted in any form or by any means, electronic, mechanical, photocopying, recording, or otherwise, without the prior written permission of Seahorse Publishing Company.

Published in the United States
Seahorse Publishing
PO Box 771325
Coral Springs, FL 33077